C0-AYJ-747

PAMPHLETS ON AMERICAN WRITERS • NUMBER 51

UNIVERSITY OF MINNESOTA

J. D. Salinger

BY JAMES E. MILLER, JR.

UNIVERSITY OF MINNESOTA PRESS • MINNEAPOLIS

Printed in the United States of America at
the North Central Publishing Company, St. Paul

Library of Congress Catalog Card Number: 65-64771

Distributed to high schools in the United States by Webster Division
McGraw-Hill Book Company
St. Louis New York San Francisco Dallas

PUBLISHED IN GREAT BRITAIN, INDIA, AND PAKISTAN BY THE OXFORD
UNIVERSITY PRESS, LONDON, BOMBAY, AND KARACHI, AND IN CANADA
BY THE COPP CLARK PUBLISHING CO. LIMITED, TORONTO

J. D. SALINGER

JAMES E. MILLER, JR., a professor of English at the University of Chicago, has served as editor of *College English,* 1960–66. He is the author or editor of many books, including *A Critical Guide to Leaves of Grass, A Reader's Guide to Herman Melville,* and *F. Scott Fitzgerald: His Art and His Technique.*

J. D. Salinger

HOLDEN CAULFIELD, the fumbling adolescent nauseated by the grossness of the world's body, may be the characteristic hero of contemporary fiction and the modern world. There can be no doubt that for today's American youth, Holden is an embodiment of their secret terrors and their accumulated hostilities, their slender joys and their magnified agonies. In his persistent innocence and his blundering virtue, he may represent to the rest of the world an adolescent America uncertainly searching for the lost garden, suspicious of alien or intimate entanglements, reluctant to encounter the horrors of reality.

No other writer since World War II has achieved the heights of popularity of J. D. (for Jerome David) Salinger. And his popularity has rested primarily on one hero, Holden Caulfield, and on one book, *The Catcher in the Rye*. Something of the intensity of the public adulation of the novelist was suggested by the appearance of his picture on the cover of *Time* magazine on September 15, 1961, together with an accompanying story that perpetuated at the same time that it extended the myth of the man and writer. Something of the depth of Salinger's academic reputation may be gauged by the publication in 1962 and 1963 of five casebooks containing source materials for use in the classroom study of Salinger. For an author born in 1919 (January 1), Salinger has excited an astonishing amount and variety of commentary by any standard of measurement. Those who have felt unmoved to appreciate have felt compelled to dissent. No writer since the 1920's — the era of Fitzgerald and Hemingway — has aroused so much public and critical interest.

But unlike Fitzgerald and Hemingway, Salinger has refused to live in public the role of American Author. The known facts of Salinger's life are sparse and undramatic. He was born in New York City the son of a Jewish father and an Irish mother, the second of two children, the first being his sister Doris. He graduated from Valley Forge Military Academy in 1936, where his I.Q. was recorded as 115. In the next few years he attended sporadically a number of colleges, including New York University, without completing a program for a degree. In 1937–38 he made a brief visit to Austria and Poland in the service of his father's meat-import business. Shortly after, he found his way into a short-story writing class taught by Whit Burnett at Columbia. In 1940, at the age of 21, he published his first story, "The Young Folks," in *Story*.

Like other young men of his generation, Salinger's perspective on life was molded by his experience in World War II. The spiritual crisis in which every Salinger hero finds himself was probably shaped, at least embryonically, in the boredom, frustrations, agonies, and horrors of the world at righteous war with itself. Salinger was drafted in 1942, was stationed for a time in Tennessee, then England (Tiverton, Devonshire), and, in 1944, landed on Utah Beach on D Day. His subsequent participation in five campaigns was surely sufficient to confirm his distaste for military experience. And if we are allowed to read any autobiography at all in his work, we may readily guess that the war was responsible for, or at least brought to the surface, an alienation from modern existence so profound as to manifest itself at times in an overpowering spiritual nausea.

Salinger began to publish stories widely during the war. He gradually moved from the little magazines to the popular mass-circulation magazines, such as *Collier's* and *Saturday Evening Post*, and finally, during the latter forties, began to publish almost exclusively in the *New Yorker*. In 1951 *The Catcher in the Rye* was published and distributed as a Book-of-the-Month Club selection; it was followed in 1953 by *Nine Stories*. Salinger married Claire Douglas, a Radcliffe graduate born in England, in 1955, and settled in Cornish, New Hampshire; two children were born, a daughter in 1955 and a son in 1960. After 1953, Salinger's productivity markedly declined. He published two slender books which brought together pairs of stories published previously in the *New Yorker*: *Franny and Zooey* (1961), containing stories first published in 1955 and 1957; and *Raise High the Roof Beam, Carpenters; and Seymour: An Introduction* (1963), with stories first published in 1955 and 1959. A prolonged silence was broken in 1965 with the publication of "Hapworth 16, 1924" in the *New Yorker*.

From 1940 to 1953, Salinger published a total of thirty stories. The rigorous selection for *Nine Stories* left twenty-one stories buried in the magazines. Although some of these stories are embarrassingly immature, others are accomplished and impressive and show an astonishingly rapid advance in craft and deepening of thematic complexity (see the bibliography for a chronological listing of the stories). The young heroines of some of these stories clearly link with the empty-headed flappers of the early F. Scott Fitzgerald, and also are forerunners of Salinger's own later and much more complex young heroines, Muriel, Esmé, Phoebe, and Franny. Some of the stories focus on young men who, however adolescent and callow and painfully innocent, are usually redeemed by the achievement of some kind of moral awareness that is both sobering and maturing; these young men are forerunners of such later characters as Holden Caulfield, Seymour Glass, and Seymour's brother Buddy. One story, a novella, worth singling out from the rest—"The Inverted Forest"—tells the tragic tale of a brilliant poet whose talent is ultimately destroyed by himself

and those about him. The poet (Raymond Fo
version of Seymour Glass, and it is worthy of
among his favorite poets are Walt Whitma
Rilke.

Some six of these early stories deal directl
would turn up again in *The Catcher in th*
("Last Day of the Last Furlough," "A Boy in
wich Has No Mayonnaise," and "The Strang
diers, Babe Gladwaller and Vincent Caulfie
and who share one characteristic—each is
most to the point of obsession, about a you
family, Babe with his sister Mattie, who fo
Phoebe, and Vincent with his kid brother H
in action. Two other stories ("I'm Crazy" a
off Madison") are in fact early versions of so
Catcher, and reveal Salinger in process of
themes and experimenting with what were
most effective techniques.

The Catcher in the Rye is a deceptively sim
book whose sources of appeal run in deep
veins. The very young are likely to identify
see the adult world in which he sojourns as
worthless; the book thus becomes a handb
guide to identification of squares. The olde
to identify with some part of the society th
see Holden as a bright but sick boy whose
ment before he can, as he will, find his ni
Holden as ideal rebel or Holden as neuroti
for either interpretation lies loosely on the
Beneath the surface lies the evidence for a
well as more convincing Holden than som
willing to recognize.

exclusively in the *New Yorker*. In 1951 *The Catcher in the Rye* was published and distributed as a Book-of-the-Month Club selection; it was followed in 1953 by *Nine Stories*. Salinger married Claire Douglas, a Radcliffe graduate born in England, in 1955, and settled in Cornish, New Hampshire; two children were born, a daughter in 1955 and a son in 1960. After 1953, Salinger's productivity markedly declined. He published two slender books which brought together pairs of stories published previously in the *New Yorker*: *Franny and Zooey* (1961), containing stories first published in 1955 and 1957; and *Raise High the Roof Beam, Carpenters; and Seymour: An Introduction* (1963), with stories first published in 1955 and 1959. A prolonged silence was broken in 1965 with the publication of "Hapworth 16, 1924" in the *New Yorker*.

From 1940 to 1953, Salinger published a total of thirty stories. The rigorous selection for *Nine Stories* left twenty-one stories buried in the magazines. Although some of these stories are embarrassingly immature, others are accomplished and impressive and show an astonishingly rapid advance in craft and deepening of thematic complexity (see the bibliography for a chronological listing of the stories). The young heroines of some of these stories clearly link with the empty-headed flappers of the early F. Scott Fitzgerald, and also are forerunners of Salinger's own later and much more complex young heroines, Muriel, Esmé, Phoebe, and Franny. Some of the stories focus on young men who, however adolescent and callow and painfully innocent, are usually redeemed by the achievement of some kind of moral awareness that is both sobering and maturing; these young men are forerunners of such later characters as Holden Caulfield, Seymour Glass, and Seymour's brother Buddy. One story, a novella, worth singling out from the rest — "The Inverted Forest" — tells the tragic tale of a brilliant poet whose talent is ultimately destroyed by himself and those about him. The poet (Raymond Ford) is clearly an early version of Seymour Glass, and it is worthy of note in passing that among his favorite poets are Walt Whitman and Rainer Maria Rilke.

Some six of these early stories deal directly with materials that would turn up again in *The Catcher in the Rye.* Four of these ("Last Day of the Last Furlough," "A Boy in France," "This Sandwich Has No Mayonnaise," and "The Stranger") present two soldiers, Babe Gladwaller and Vincent Caulfield, who are buddies and who share one characteristic—each is deeply concerned, almost to the point of obsession, about a younger member of his family, Babe with his sister Mattie, who foreshadows Esmé and Phoebe, and Vincent with his kid brother Holden, who is missing in action. Two other stories ("I'm Crazy" and "Slight Rebellion off Madison") are in fact early versions of some of the episodes in *Catcher,* and reveal Salinger in process of discovering his major themes and experimenting with what were to develop into his most effective techniques.

The Catcher in the Rye is a deceptively simple, enormously rich book whose sources of appeal run in deep and complexly varied veins. The very young are likely to identify with Holden and to see the adult world in which he sojourns as completely phony and worthless; the book thus becomes a handbook for rebels and a guide to identification of squares. The older generation is likely to identify with some part of the society that is satirized, and to see Holden as a bright but sick boy whose psyche needs adjustment before he can, as he will, find his niche and settle down. Holden as ideal rebel or Holden as neurotic misfit—the evidence for either interpretation lies loosely on the surface of the novel. Beneath the surface lies the evidence for a more complicated as well as more convincing Holden than some of his admirers are willing to recognize.

A brief summary of *Catcher* suggests the episodic nature of its structure. Holden Caulfield flunks out of Pencey Prep in Pennsylvania and starts out on the terrible journey to his home in New York, where he must face his parents after this latest in a series of expulsions. The journey becomes a combination nightmare and burlesque where horror and comedy mix in inexplicable fashion. Holden has a series of encounters with people, but never a genuine engagement (as he observes, "People never give your message to anybody"). His roommate at Pencey, Stradlater, is a clean-cut youth but a "secret slob." The boy next door, Ackley, is a slob in public – but still can provide occasional company for a lonely Holden. On the train to New York, Holden meets the mother of one of his classmates – and lies "like a madman" to reassure her of her illusions about her "sensitive" son ("That guy . . . was about as sensitive as a goddam toilet seat"). In the big city he calls a faded name he pulls out of his wallet – a former burlesque stripper, Faith Cavendish – and has a talk but does not connect. He drifts into the company of three female tourists, all naive greenhorns, in a nightclub – and gets stuck for the entire evening's bill. At another nightclub he runs into a "boring" friend of his older brother, D. B. (now "prostituting" himself by writing for the movies), and escapes ("People are always ruining things for you") . Back at his hotel, he acquiesces in a suggestion from the elevator "guy" and is visited in his room by Sunny; but feeling "more depressed than sexy," he tells her he isn't in the mood and attempts to pay her off with the agreed-on price of five dollars – when she demands ten, a demand backed up by the fists of the brutish elevator boy, Maurice. So ends the first day of Holden's odyssey.

On the next day, Sunday, the journey begins again, but with a new cast of characters. Holden's first encounter at breakfast is a pleasant one, with two nuns to whom he insists on giving ten of his few remaining dollars. Holden then begins to drift with the day. He passes a poor, Sunday-dressed family, whose little boy is singing "If a body catch a body coming through the rye"; he walks over to his beloved Museum of Natural History ("everything always stayed right where it was"), but decides not to go in. In the afternoon, he takes his old girl friend, Sally Hayes, to see the Lunts in a play (both turn out to be phony), quarrels with her over his proposal to run away, and is left alone. Next he goes to Radio City Music Hall and sees a phony movie, after which he meets Carl Luce, an old schoolmate now at Columbia, who is a specialist on "flits" (Holden asks him, "What're you majoring in? . . . Perverts?"). Left alone again (Holden seems always to be left alone when he is most lonesome), Holden gets drunk, calls Sally, is rebuffed, and finally goes home to his sister Phoebe, alone in the family apartment. After a challenge from Phoebe to name something he likes, and after he finally settles on being a catcher in the rye, keeping the little kids from falling over "some crazy cliff," Holden goes over to stay the night with his former English teacher, Mr. Antolini, arriving in the Antolini apartment just after the end of a drinking party. Mr. Antolini talks like a father to Holden, quoting Wilhelm Stekel on the meaning of genuine maturity, "The mark of the immature man is that he wants to die nobly for a cause, while the mark of the mature man is that he wants to live humbly for one." After drifting off to sleep on the Antolini couch, Holden awakens in fright to find Mr. Antolini patting him on the head. He quickly concocts some clumsy excuse about getting his bags, and runs from this threatening show of affection – that may be "something perverty."

As Holden leaves the Antolini apartment, the light of Monday morning is brightening the sky. But his only thought is to execute immediately his plan to run off to the West. He writes Phoebe a note at school to meet him at noon near the Metropolitan Museum, and, as he is waiting for her, he visits the depths of the

Egyptian tomb. He feels sick, passes out briefly, and then recovers, to go out to meet Phoebe. She has come to run away with him, but he tells her that she must stay at home, that he isn't going anywhere anyway. They visit the zoo, watch the bears briefly, and then go to the carrousel. As she rides round and round on the carrousel, Holden makes up his mind to stay, to quit running; and, in the middle of a drenching rain, as he watches Phoebe go around in her endless circle on the carrousel, he begins to feel "so damn happy" that he ends up "damn near bawling."

This skeleton of events in *Catcher* distorts the book considerably, and demonstrates how dependent it is on incidental detail, what might even be called plot irrelevancies, for its most moving and profound meanings. Such detail and such crucially relevant irrelevancies are woven into the book's very texture. Salinger is able to achieve this loose-seeming yet tightly woven structure through ingenious exploitation of his chosen point of view. Like Mark Twain in *Huckleberry Finn,* Salinger appears to have hit upon the perfect way of telling the tale – or of letting the tale tell itself. Holden speaks out in his own idiom, and although his clichés belong to us all, the intonation and gesture are his own – and they strike home. Moreover, Salinger carefully places Holden on the psychiatrist's couch in California, apparently on the way to some kind of recovery from his spiritual collapse (we learn on the opening page of the novel that D. B. may be driving him home the next month). This allows Holden a free play of mind around the events he recounts, enabling him to see them from a more objective perspective than he could possibly have had during their actual happening, and enabling him also to move back beyond those three critical days into his past in recollection of more distant excursions, encounters, and collisions that seem somehow to have a bearing on his predicament. This point of view results in the novel's marvelous richness of texture.

As the Holden on his journey is re-created for us by the Holden on the psychiatrist's couch, we recognize that the journey is more than movement through space — it is a movement, also, from innocence to knowledge, from self-ignorance to self-awareness, from isolation to involvement. For example, in the episode in which Holden urges Sally Hayes to run off with him, and she balks, he tells her, "You give me a royal pain in the ass, if you want to know the truth." In the midst of his "madman" apologies, Sally's somewhat pompous indignation undermines his serious intention, and he laughs. The narrator Holden comments: "I have one of these very loud, stupid laughs. I mean if I ever sat behind myself in a movie or something, I'd probably lean over and tell myself to please shut up. It made old Sally madder than ever." In retrospect Holden is able to see what he only half comprehended when he was with Sally — that he shares the responsibility for this one more failure in his frantic attempt to communicate with people and break out of his isolation. In his retrospective examination of the episode, Holden says: "If you want to know the truth, I don't even know why I started all that stuff with her. . . . I probably wouldn't've taken her even if she'd wanted to go with me." Holden thus penetrates to his own deception and his own phoniness, and is one more step on the way to the kind of involved awareness that will enable him at the end, after he has finished reconstructing his tale, to say: "About all I know is, I sort of *miss* everybody I told about." This knowledge, though it is casually presented in the closing lines of the book, is a difficult, profound, and mature knowledge that lies at the novel's center of gravity. It involves both a recognition that there can be no self-monopoly of innocence and a discovery that there can be no shield from complicity.

Holden's quest, then, may be stated in a number of ways. In one sense, his quest is a quest to preserve an innocence that is in peril of vanishing — the innocence of childhood, the spotless innocence of a self horrified at contamination in the ordinary and inevitable involvements of life. In another sense, the quest is a quest for an ideal but un-human love that will meet all demands but make none; a relationship so sensitively attuned that all means of communication, however subtle, will remain alertly open, and all the messages, in whatever language, will get through. Perhaps in its profoundest sense Holden's quest is a quest for identity, a search for the self — he does, for example, go through a number of guises, such as Rudolf Schmidt when he talks with his classmate's mother or Jim Steele when he is visited by the prostitute Sunny. But he remains, however he might wish to the contrary, Holden Caulfield, and the self he is led to discover is Holden's and none other. And that self he discovers is a human self and an involved self that cannot, finally, break what Hawthorne once called the "magnetic chain of humanity"; he cannot deny the love within him when he begins to miss all the people, "bastards" included, he has told about.

Holden vacillates throughout *Catcher* between the imperative of involvement and revulsion at involvement, and the result is a dual series of compelling images that act as magnets that both attract and repel. He is driven first to make some connection; like Whitman's "Noiseless Patient Spider," Holden launches forth filament after filament, but his "gossamer thread" never catches anywhere — until at the end it catches Phoebe in an entangled web from which Holden is obligated to release her. At the same time that he is casting forth, out of the agony of his loneliness, the filaments spun from his soul, Holden is repelled to the point of nausea (he is frequently about to puke or vomit) by the fundamental physicality of the human predicament. This inescapable physicality is a phenomenon of all human relationships, all human situations, by their very nature of being human. It is this terrible knowledge to which Holden must reconcile himself. Even a casual relationship with a schoolmate is heavily colored and shaped by the individual's imprisonment in his physical identity. For instance, Ackley's teeth are mossy-looking, his face is pimpled, and his room is filled with a "funny stink" – all matters of acute painfulness for Holden to adjust to when in the desperation of his isolation he seeks out Ackley for companionship (launching forth a filament). It is in a context of this kind that Holden's attitude toward sex, that most intense form of all human involvement, must be placed in order to comprehend both the fascination and the fear that he feels at its invocation. This ambivalence is portrayed vividly in the episode in which Holden looks out of his New York hotel window and is confronted by a series of scenes of sexual tragicomedy (an episode functionally reminiscent of the humanity-embroiled prison episode in Graham Greene's *The Power and the Glory*), and comments: "The trouble was, that kind of junk is sort of fascinating to watch, even if you don't want it to be. . . . Sometimes I can think of *very* crumby stuff I wouldn't mind doing if the opportunity came up." The insight is penetrating, and the understanding is a step beyond wisdom.

Just as one part of Holden drives him forward in his painful quest for some responsive relationship with people, in spite of the terror of the physical, another and deeper part urges his withdrawal and flight, and even the ultimate disengagement of death – the utter abandonment of physicality. A controlling image in this sequence is that of the abandoned ducks on the frozen lagoon in Central Park. Obviously Holden repeatedly sees his own plight symbolized by the forlorn and freezing ducks. Another image that recurs is Holden's dead brother Allie's baseball mitt, in which are inscribed the poems of Emily Dickinson (a poet whose dominant subject was death). Again and again, Holden (like Emily Dickinson) imagines his own death, as, for example, after the degrading incident with the hotel pimp and the prostitute: "What I really felt like, though, was committing suicide. I felt like jumping out the window. I probably would've done it, too, if I'd been sure somebody'd cover me up as soon as I landed." The tone of levity betrays just how deep the suicidal impulse is lodged—to surge again on later occasions dangerously near to the surface. Holden's fascinated interest in the Museum of Natural History, particularly in those human scenes (a squaw, an Eskimo) statically preserved behind glass, where nobody moves and nothing changes, no matter how many times you come back—this intense interest is clearly related in some subterranean way to his deepest instincts. And when Phoebe challenges Holden to name something he really likes, the only response he at first can make is to name the dead—his brother Allie; or James Castle, the boy who was teased by his schoolmates into committing suicide by jumping out the dormitory window.

On one level, *The Catcher in the Rye* may be read as a story of death and rebirth. It is symbolically relevant that the time of year is deep winter: it is the time of Christmas, a season of expiration and parturition. Holden is fated, at the critical age of sixteen years, to fall from innocence, to experience the death of the old self and to arise a new Holden to confront the world afresh—much like Ishmael and his symbolic immersion and resurrection at the end of *Moby Dick*. The metaphor of the fall is sounded again and again in the closing pages of the novel. Holden himself introduces it, when talking with Phoebe, in his vision of himself as the catcher in the rye. His own stance at the edge of the cliff, is, in fact, precarious; ironically he is unable to prevent his own imminent fall. Mr. Antolini sounds the warning for Holden, directly and fervently, when he tells him that he is heading for "a terrible, terrible fall," and adds: "This fall I think you're riding for—it's a special kind of fall, a horrible kind. The man falling isn't permitted to feel or hear himself hit bottom. He just keeps falling and falling." It is only a short while after this warning that Holden awakens to find Mr. Antolini patting him on the head, abandons in panic this last refuge open to him, and starts to run – or fall – again. The precise motives behind Mr. Antolini's odd, but very human, gesture are obscure, as Holden himself comes shortly to realize: his patting Holden's head is, in its context, certainly a suggestive physical act; but it is also, surely, an act of profound, human, non-sexual affection, a gesture of the spirit as much as of the hand. Mr. Antolini's motives (he has been drinking) are no doubt muddled in his own mind. But Holden's shrinking back in horror from this physical touch, his immediate assumption that Mr. Antolini is a "flit" on the make, betrays his revulsion at the inevitable mixture of the dark and the light in any human act – a mixture inevitable because of the inescapable *physicality* of the human condition. It is from this level of lofty innocence that Holden is doomed to fall.

Holden's running from the Antolini apartment takes him some distance, indeed, on the way in his fall from innocence. He begins to realize that he has made a mistake, that he has misjudged Mr. Antolini, or has been too cold and severe in his behavior; and he becomes depressed and "screwed up" as he recalls that it was Mr. Antolini who had picked up the dead boy, James Castle, after he committed suicide. As Holden walks along the street in a critical state, something "spooky" begins to happen. He recalls: "Every time I came to the end of a block and stepped off the goddam curb, I had this feeling that I'd never get to the other side of the street. I thought I'd just go down, down, down, and nobody'd ever see me again." His sensation of falling is counterbalanced by his fantasy of flight to the Far West where he will become a deaf-mute, cut off from the world in a kind of living death, his innocence desperately preserved. But the real world, the terribly physical world, continues to press in – and down – on him. At Phoebe's school, he rubs out one obscenity only to be confronted with another,

scratched deeply into the wall. He decides, "If you had a million years to do it in, you couldn't rub out even *half* the 'Fuck You' signs in the world. It's impossible." Holden is thus close to realizing the futility of any attempt to be a catcher in the rye: the kids cannot, in the world as it is, be shielded from the crazy cliff. While waiting at the Metropolitan Museum for Phoebe, Holden descends into the Egyptian tomb, where he finds it "nice and peaceful" — until he notices the obscenity once more, scrawled in red crayon, "under the glass part of the wall." He then imagines his own tombstone, displaying under his own name the revolting words of the obscenity.

At this point, Holden's horror and his dream, his revulsion at the world and his fantasy of death, come together in the image of his tombstone and he finds himself confronting the critical moment of decision — life or death; the world with all its obscenities or suicide with all its denials. The image of the tombstone bearing the obscenity suggests that suicide itself would be a kind of ultimate capitulation to the terrible physicality of life, an ironic involvement of the flesh at the very moment of abdication of the flesh. Death thus becomes not a gesture of defiance but of surrender. Holden feels both nausea and faintness, and he actually passes out momentarily, and falls to the floor, a final fall that marks the end of the descent. When he arises, he feels better; the crisis is past, the choice for life symbolically made, the slow ascent begun. Phoebe's spontaneous generosity expressed in her willingness to run away with him confirms his decision to stay, to become involved, and to rejoin the human race. In the closing pages of the novel, as he watches Phoebe, in her blue coat, go around and around on the carrousel, Holden becomes afraid that as she grabs for the gold ring, she will fall, but he restrains himself: "The thing with kids is, if they want to grab for the gold ring, you have to let them do it, and not say anything. If they fall off, they fall off, but it's bad if you say anything to them." Gone now is the dream of being the catcher in the rye. Whether in the fields of rye, or on the circular carrousel, children must eventually fall, as Holden has fallen. Holden can be happy — "so damn happy" — now in the knowledge that Phoebe is held by the magic and endless circle of the carrousel in a suspended state of perfect and impenetrable innocence; and his happiness can be intensified and rendered poignant in the mature awareness that the state is momentary, that the music will stop and the magic circle break, that the fall, finally, cannot be stayed. (It may be worth noting, parenthetically, that one of Salinger's favorite poets, Rilke, has a poem entitled "The Carrousel," in which there is a "little blue girl," and in which the carrousel "circles and turns and has no goal.")

For all its seriousness, *Catcher in the Rye* is one of the funniest books in American literature, and much has been said relating its humor to the native American tradition, and particularly to Mark Twain's *Huckleberry Finn*. Perhaps of equal importance with its connections to the past is the role of *Catcher* in the development of the post-World War II "black" humor, the humor that has occasional elements of irresponsibility, cruelty, despair, and insanity. Examples are Wright Morris' *Ceremony in Lone Tree* (1960), Joseph Heller's *Catch-22* (1961), and Ken Kesey's *One Flew over the Cuckoo's Nest* (1962). One small episode in *Catcher* will suggest its place in this new direction of contemporary American humor. After leaving the Antolini apartment, as Holden is wandering in a daze about the streets, he comes upon a small vignette that seems to sum up the weird incongruities of modern life as he has encountered it: ". . . I passed these two guys that were unloading this big Christmas tree off a truck. One guy kept saying to the other guy, 'Hold the sonuvabitch *up*! Hold it *up*, for Chrissake!' It certainly was a gorgeous way to talk about a Christmas tree. It was sort of funny, though, in an awful way, and I started to sort of laugh. It was about the *worst* thing I could've done, because the minute I started to laugh I thought I was going to vomit. I really did, I even started to, but it went away. I don't know why." It is, of course, *for the sake of Christ* that the tree has been reaped and hauled and now put into place. But the mover's remark, "Hold it *up,* for Chrissake," is only ironically and absurdly an invocation of this now lost original meaning, embedded like a fossil in language—the language not of a blessing but of a curse.

Absurdity, nausea—these terms seem recurrently relevant to Holden's predicament as he hangs suspended between laughter and sickness. And is not Holden's predicament in some sense the modern predicament? At one point he remarks: ". . . I'm sort of glad they've got the atomic bomb invented. If there's ever another war, I'm going to sit right the hell on top of it. I'll volunteer for it, I swear to God I will." Perhaps the post-World War II comedy of blackness points the way of endurance in an insanely reeling world: if we do not at times feel nausea at contemporary horrors, we are, in a way, already dead; if we cannot occasionally laugh at contemporary absurdities, we shall in the darkness of our despair soon die.

The chasteness of the title *Nine Stories* (1953) is in line with the severity of the selection. The stories Salinger chose are late stories, published between 1948 and 1953—all, with two exceptions, in the *New Yorker.* Although the tales in *Nine Stories* are arranged in the order of their publication (see the bibliography), it is illuminating to look at them in a series of thematic groupings. Before rearranging the order, however, it is useful to note that the opening and closing stories of the volume portray violent deaths, the first (Seymour Glass's) a certain suicide, the second (Teddy's) a foreseen "accident." It is possible that the nature of the one death may help in understanding the other. Indeed, there are thematic echoes and reverberations throughout *Nine Stories* which give the volume a singleness of impact which belies its multiplicity.

The dominant theme which recurs, in richly varied thematic contexts, is alienation, an alienation which may conclude in some kind of reconciliation or accommodation, but which may also result in distortion of the soul, bitterness, nausea, and the ultimate withdrawal into death. The causes of the alienation are frequently obscure but always complex. Sometimes society seems at fault, in the horrors of racial prejudice or the horrors of war. But sometimes the fault seems to lie in a failure of personal relationships — the filament (of Whitman's spider) is launched, but does not catch; or caught, does not hold. Sometimes, however, the cause of alienation lies deeply within, in a turbulence of the spirit — plunging the individual into a dark night of the soul, or dazzling him in the ecstasy of a vision of mystical union — two radically different states that mystics have always found in close conjunction.

"Down at the Dinghy" (which holds the center position in *Nine Stories*) is the single story in the volume dealing directly with a social issue — racial prejudice; a young boy, four-year-old Lionel Tannenbaum, has heard a housekeeper call his father a "kike," and has run away to the family dinghy, from which his mother (who is, incidentally, Boo Boo Glass) finally coaxes him — discovering, ironically, that he thought a kike "one of those things that go up in the *air*" (a kite).

Several stories are tales of estrangement in love, both premarital and marital. Perhaps the most optimistic of these is "Just before the War with the Eskimos": a sensitive, perceptive young man (Franklin Graff) who has been kept out of the war — and somewhat out of life — because of a bad "ticker," has drifted into an unwholesome relationship with what appears to be a homosexual; when Ginnie Mannox comes home with his sister one day, the young man launches forth a filament that appears to catch (he had written eight letters to Ginnie's sister that went unanswered), and she accepts his zany offer of a leftover chicken sandwich and leaves determined to come back. "The Laughing Man" describes the sad end rather than the happy beginning of a relationship: John Gedsudski, a young law student, is in charge of a group of young boys (the Comanches), and keeps them entertained between ballgames by narrating an endless tale about a kind of deformed Robin Hood (with a "hairless, pecan-shaped head and a face that featured . . . an enormous oval cavity below the nose"); when the young man's relationship with Mary Hudson blossoms, and she even participates in the ballgames, the plot of his tale proliferates with great energy and gusto, but when they quarrel and part (no cause is given), he bitterly describes the brutal captivity and death of his "laughing man," unforgettably shocking his young Comanches.

Two stories describe marital estrangement and betrayal. "Uncle Wiggily in Connecticut" portrays a gray flannel world in which a suburban housewife, Eloise, drinking with an old school chum, gradually reveals the hidden source of her antagonism toward her daughter (who has a naughty imaginary playmate) and her indifference toward her husband: she recalls with alcoholic vividness her old love (his name is Walt Glass) killed during the war in Japan by the absurd explosion of a toy Japanese stove. "Pretty Mouth and Green My Eyes" is an urbanized tale of the managerial set and consists of two telephone conversations that take place after a cocktail party, initiated each time by a junior executive to a superior in the same firm, the first to inquire whether the older man saw the younger's wife leave the party, the second to explain that the wife has just come home; but the irony is that the wife is in bed with the older man even as he takes the two calls.

But Salinger's best stories portray an alienation more profound and more unsettling than that produced by the shock of racial prejudice or the shock of the failure of love. The most celebrated example of this more ambiguous alienation is found in "For Esmé — with Love and Squalor," a tale of war and spiritual crisis told by the protagonist some six healing years after the searing events. But the events remain so vividly painful that the narrator must envelop them in anonymity and must remove them from himself by placing them in the third person. In England during the war, in training for duty in Europe, the narrator meets and has tea with thirteen-year-old Esmé and her five-year-old brother Charles, and discovers a moment of human warmth and sanity to relieve the dreariness and insanity of camp life in wartime. Esmé is all the more endearing for the mature role she has bravely assumed in her family after the death of her father, slain in North Africa. The scene shifts to occupied Bavaria after five campaigns (and V-E Day), and the narration suddenly shifts into the third person. Sergeant X, feeling "his mind dislodge itself and teeter, like insecure luggage on an overhead rack," picks up from the table a book by Goebbels entitled *Die Zeit Ohne Beispiel* ("The Unprecedented Era"), once owned by a low-ranking Nazi that X himself had arrested, and finds written in it, "Dear God, life is hell." Sergeant X writes under this inscription a quotation from Dostoevski: "Fathers and teachers, I ponder 'What is hell?' I maintain that it is the suffering of being unable to love."

It is precisely this hell that Sergeant X is experiencing, as is immediately demonstrated by the intrusion of his companion on the five campaigns, Corporal Z, an insensitive, vacuous individual whose very physical presence — belches, brick-red slicked-down hair, overdecorated uniform, and all — is overwhelming. Corporal Z's brutalized, dehumanized conversation at this moment of spiritual crisis, especially his casual recollection of the cat he cruelly and meaninglessly shot while with his buddy during a moment of battle tension, triggers the revulsion in Sergeant X that causes him immediately to vomit. But a sickness of the soul — the sickness of being unable to love — cannot be regurgitated. Left alone, Sergeant X aimlessly looks through his mail and finds a package that turns out to contain a letter from Esmé together with her father's watch which she had been wearing on their first and only encounter. The letter and watch are like a fresh breeze that blows through and cleanses the sickroom of the soul. They provide an illumination that renews and refreshes Sergeant X's darkened spirit, as he once again — in the presence, however remote, of such innocent affection — feels himself able to love. He had, perhaps, in his nausea at humanity, been near suicide; the watch that Esmé sent him restored to him a reservoir of time that he had been on the verge of losing forever.

"De Daumier-Smith's Blue Period" tells the story of a young man, at loose ends with life, who obtains a job as an instructor at a Canadian correspondence art school, run by a Japanese man and his wife; among his mediocre students is a talented nun who attracts his attention and to whom he writes a long, almost intimate letter, which precipitates the nun's withdrawal from the course; shortly after, the school is closed down for being improperly licensed and De Daumier-Smith returns to his former life to pick up the threads he had cut. Of course, the story is much more than this bare outline shows. The episode is the crucial, formative experience in the protagonist's life, but it is, fundamentally, an experience of the spirit. The young man, who narrates his own story, is a kind of Ishmael at the beginning, his mother dead, his stepfather providing a tenuous hotel existence in New York; he is sickened by the multitudes of people in the city, prays to be alone, and suddenly discovers that everything he touches turns to "solid loneliness." It is out of a mixture of frustration and desperation that he applies for the art school job in Canada under the fantastic name of De Daumier-Smith — in search of a new identity.

The thematic focal point of the story is an orthopedic appliances shop underneath the second-floor art school. There two incidents occur, one "hideous" (a dark night), the other "transcendent" (an illumination), that determine the fate of the narrator. After he has mailed his long, adulatory letter to the nun about her work, even suggesting that he visit her, and is living in a kind of exalted anticipation of her reply, he pauses one evening before the window of the shop and is inexplicably plunged into gloom: "The thought was forced on me that no matter how coolly or sensibly or gracefully I might one day learn to live my life, I would always at best be a visitor in a garden of enamel urinals and bedpans, with a sightless, wooden dummy-deity standing by in a marked-down rupture truss." The thought is unendurable, and De Daumier-Smith rushes off to bed and forces his mind to envision a visit with the nun at her convent, in a relationship "without sin" but in a purity of image "too ecstatic to hold in place."

After receiving word that the nun has been withdrawn from the art course, De Daumier-Smith is depressed, angrily writes letters dismissing his other students, and goes out for a walk – only to pause once again before the terrible window. This time there is a girl in a "green, yellow and lavender" dress in the window changing the truss on the wooden dummy; when she sees the narrator, she becomes flustered, starts to exit, and falls on her bottom (recalling the "buttocks to buttocks" bus scene in New York earlier in the story). As De Daumier-Smith reaches out to help her, his fingers are stopped by the glass of the window – and the "Experience" occurs: "Suddenly . . . the sun came up and sped toward the bridge of my nose at the rate of ninety-three million miles a second. Blinded and very frightened – I had to put my hand on the glass to keep my balance. The thing lasted for no more than a few seconds. When I got my sight back, the girl had gone from the window, leaving behind her a shimmering field of exquisite, twice-blessed, enamel flowers." In spite of the narrator's protests, the incident has all the elements of some kind of "genuine mysticism." De Daumier-Smith's mystic response to the girl in the window is reminiscent of Stephen Dedalus' reaction to his glimpse of the wading girl in *A Portrait of the Artist as a Young Man*—a glimpse that deflected him from priesthood and sent him out to encounter the world. The narrator, in returning to his former life, is symbolically rejoining the human race; he has made the decision to become more than just a "visitor" in the physical universe.

In "Teddy," Salinger carries experimentation in mystical fiction about as far as it can be carried without entering the realm of fantasy, and even in "Teddy" there are elements of the fantastic. Ten-year-old Theodore McArdle, on an ocean voyage with his irritable, quarreling parents and his six-year-old sister (who, he says, doesn't like him), is gradually revealed to us as the most remarkable child in Salinger's large gallery of remarkable children. He holds the Vedantic theory of reincarnation, and believes that in his last incarnation he was "making very nice spiritual advancement." He had his first mystical experience at an early age: "I was six when I saw that everything was God, and my hair stood up . . . It was on a Sunday, I remember. My sister was only a very tiny child then, and she was drinking her milk, and all of a sudden I saw that *she* was God and the *milk* was God. I mean, all she was doing was pouring God into God, if you know what I mean." But perhaps Teddy's most marvelous gift is his intuitive grasp of the future—not clairvoyance, but a sense of the need for increased awareness or concern at certain potentially hazardous times. He writes in his diary: "It will either happen today or February 14, 1958 when I am sixteen. It is ridiculous to mention even." The reference, we find out later, is to his own death. In his final conversation with a fellow passenger, the teacher Bob Nicholson, he says that death is a minor matter, really ("All you do is get the heck out of your body when you die"), and that it could happen to him that very day—say, for example, if he went down to the swimming pool, found it empty, and was pushed in by his small sister (who, after all, "hasn't been a human being for very many lives"). As events turn out, this is precisely what happens, as Nicholson realizes on his way following Teddy down to the pool—when he suddenly hears the piercing scream of Teddy's sister, no doubt hysterical in fear and horror at what she has done.

If we accept the world created by Salinger in this story, we do not mourn for Teddy, but recognize that he is on his way to another incarnation, and closer in the cycle that will bring him to the final and permanent meditation with God. In the story, Salinger was probably experimenting with rather than expressing belief, and the tale should be accepted in that spirit. More important, however, than Teddy's gift of intuitive foresight are his desire for meditation, his dislike of sentimentality, and his distaste for logic. It is through periodical retreat and meditation that he is able to achieve his remarkable knowledge—or make "spiritual advancement." Poetry and love are too frequently destroyed by sentimentality; thus Teddy prefers Japanese poetry (" 'Nothing in the voice of the cicada intimates how soon it will die' "), and thus he loves God ("If *I* were God, I certainly wouldn't want people to love me sentimentally"). Adam brought logic into the world by his eating of the apple, and man has been an apple-eater ever since; man must "vomit" up this "logic and intellectual stuff" if he ever wants "to see things as they really are" (the language here—especially the image of vomiting—is revealing as it relates to the recurring nausea in Salinger's heroes). After man has emptied himself of the "intellectual stuff," he might, through meditation, be able to get back the conscious knowledge that he has somehow lost. ("I grew my own body. . . . Nobody else did it for me. So if I grew it, I must have known *how* to grow it. Unconsciously, at least. I may have lost the *con*scious knowledge of how to grow it sometime in the last few hundred thousand years, but the knowledge is still *there* . . .") Whatever we may think of Teddy—and I think that we must accept him (if necessary through willing suspension of disbelief) as a genuine mystic, spiritually advanced far beyond the general level of this world, operating on the very highest levels of cosmic consciousness—it is clear that he is too much for this world to contain. Like Melville's Billy Budd with his colossal innocence, Teddy with his staggering spirituality must die, as he himself seems to understand, before he unsettles society from its foundations.

The opening tale of *Nine Stories,* "A Perfect Day for Bananafish," gains in meaning in the light of all the stories that follow it. Moreover, as it presents a crucial episode in the saga of Seymour Glass, discussion of it may well stand as a prologue to treatment of Salinger's longer and later stories devoted to the Glass family. Of the seven children of Bessie and Les Glass, three appear in *Nine Stories*—Boo Boo, the third of the children, is the mother in "Down at the Dinghy," Walt, one of the twins who came fourth, is the remembered dead soldier and lover in "Uncle Wiggily in Connecticut," and Seymour, the first of them all and the family guru, is the central character of "A Perfect Day for Bananafish." There are two major scenes in the story, the first in which Muriel Glass talks long distance from Florida with her mother in New York about the peculiar behavior of Muriel's husband Seymour, and the second in which Seymour out on the beach takes little Sybil Carpenter on her float into the water and talks with her about any number of things—including bananafish. At the end of the story, Seymour walks into the hotel room where Muriel lies sleeping and puts a bullet in his temple.

To assume that Seymour is simply a psychotic is to render the story meaningless. To interpret his suicide as his simple and direct device to sever his marriage to a vacuous, spiritually shallow girl is to reduce the story to the dimensions of the daily tabloid. Although Seymour's suicide is explored in some detail in the later Glass stories, it is possible, as it should be, to read the story without the later amplifications and discover a Seymour who is not inconsistent with the Seymour of the later books. In the conversation between Muriel and her mother, along with its expression of a faddish and naive faith in psychoanalysis, several hints about Seymour's behavior are dropped but left unexplained. For example, Seymour has apparently had some kind of obsession about trees, repeatedly stares at them, and has apparently run his father-in-law's car into one. A Freudian critic might well see phallic significance in this obsession, and it would be hard to deny that the tree has some such suggestion. But the obsession is surely more complex than such an interpretation allows. Seymour's fascination for trees may well be born of his intuitive grasp of the tree's deep and enduring natural knowledge of its place and its role (as Teddy would say, it knows unconsciously how to grow and how to be).

Although Seymour shares with Holden Caulfield and Sergeant X an acute sensitivity, ranging from revulsion to ecstasy, to the physicality of the world, his Sybil does not serve (as Phoebe and Esmé serve their young men) to deflect him from self-destruction (although she does, as a kind of inverted sibyl, young rather than ancient, confirm his deepest intuitions). Nor does Seymour seem to have the agitation of Holden or the nausea of Sergeant X. Seymour displays, rather, a tragic resignation. His story of the bananafish that swims into the hole and consumes bananas until he is too fat to come out, and therefore must die, is a paradigm of his own situation. He is a bananafish, not because he has indulged his senses to the point of grossness, but rather because of his keen sensitivity to the overwhelming physicality of existence — his senses have been ravaged by the physical world, and he has found himself entrapped and must die. His figurative fatness might well be another man's real leanness. When we observe Muriel, at the opening of the story, reading an article called "Sex Is Fun – or Hell" (rather than the poetry of Rilke, for example, which Seymour has recommended), we come to sense that for the Glasses sex must be hell: Seymour's surfeit would be for Muriel a kind of abstention.

When Seymour leaves Sybil, he kisses the arch of her foot; immediately after, on the elevator, he angrily accuses a woman of sneaking a look at his feet. This keen sensitivity about the feet epitomizes Seymour's attitude toward the physical. The kiss for him represents symbolically the glut of any number of bananas; a glance (or apparent glance) from a stranger at this intimate and sensitive physical embodiment of the self becomes extremely painful, so painful that continued physical existence is unendurable. When he walks into the bedroom, the only sense operative is the sense of smell: he is overwhelmed by the odor of the "new calfskin luggage and nail-lacquer remover." Even at the end, his senses remain glutted. Seymour Glass can *see more* (in trees, for instance) because he has begun to vomit up the apple of logic, and possess, like Teddy, a magnified spiritual consciousness. Every physical fact has become a virtual spiritual maze. But sadly, those about him can think only of his "maladjustment" and his possible "cure" through psychoanalysis (precisely the thing, according to Zooey later, that precipitated the suicide). As it is painful for Seymour to see anyone mean to a dog, he would not kill himself to hurt Muriel. On the contrary, his suicide is a release for her to engage life again at a level she can apprehend, and a release for himself from a physicality that has simply ceased to be endurable. It is the only escape from his bananahole.

After *Nine Stories*, Salinger's imagination appears to have been completely absorbed by the Glass family; and in spite of Seymour's suicide, he remains a dominant presence throughout. Although "Franny" and "Zooey" were published as two separate stories in the *New Yorker*, they make a remarkably unified novel. Franny, youngest of the Glasses' seven children, goes to visit her college boyfriend, Lane Coutell, at his Ivy League school, where the plans call for lunch at the posh local restaurant, attendance at the football game, and a general good time (there are several hints that they are sleeping together). But over martinis, as Lane talks about the success of one of his papers on Flaubert's testicularity (a Freudian analysis which he might try to publish), and as Franny talks about her disillusionment with all her professors, who are pedants and phonies, she suddenly excuses herself, goes to the ladies' room, and gives way to a violent fit of trembling and tears. When she returns, Lane notices the little pea-green book in her purse, and she begins to talk about it – *The Way of a Pilgrim* – and a form of prayer recommended in it, involving an endless repetition of the Jesus prayer – "Lord Jesus Christ, have mercy on me." As Franny tries to explain how the prayer is supposed to work, Lane expresses his skepticism (". . . all those religious experiences have a very obvious psychological background"), and Franny is swept up again in a wave of nausea, this time passing out in the restaurant. She comes to in the manager's office, she concurs in Lane's plans for a quiet afternoon of rest, and as she is left alone at the end her lips are moving with a repetition of the Jesus prayer.

The narration shifts from third to first person in "Zooey," but the narrator, Buddy Glass, introduces himself only to fade behind the third person again soon after. The scene shifts to the Glass family apartment in New York, where the mother Bessie and the sixth of the seven Glass children, a television actor, Zooey, are ministering to the needs of Franny, now home and languishing on the living room couch. There are three major scenes, all domestic, in "Zooey." The first takes place in the family bathroom, where

Zooey is first discovered in the tub rereading a four-year-old letter from his older brother Buddy; the room is invaded by Bessie, bent on enlisting Zooey's help in succoring the sick child Franny. In the bantering conversation that ensues, surely the longest bathroom scene in all literature, Bessie's general density and particularly her reliance on psychoanalysis indicates that she is making the usual mistake in analyzing the soul-sickness of her children. In the next scene, Zooey goes to the living room where he gradually and gently lures Franny out of her shell and then tries to shock her out of her sickness by describing to her her "little stink of piousness" and the "little snotty crusade" she is "leading against everybody." The shock merely intensifies Franny's anguish, and Zooey retreats, this time to the sacrosanct room once occupied by Seymour and Buddy Glass and which still has the phone listed in Seymour's name. There, after a period of communion with Seymour's spirit, Zooey, a handkerchief over his mouth to disguise his voice, calls Franny over the sacred phone, and she takes the call in her parents' bedroom. On Seymour's phone pretending to be Buddy, Zooey finally wins his way to Franny's understanding; she discovers that she is speaking with Zooey, but she continues to listen, and is at last persuaded to eat Bessie's "consecrated chicken soup," and to return to her theater activities – in short, to rejoin the human race. At the end, Franny is suffused with an inexplicable joy that causes her to smile just before falling into a "deep, dreamless sleep" – clearly the sleep of renewal and resuscitation.

The pattern that Franny follows, from nausea to joy, from withdrawal to return, is the familiar one in Salinger, as witness Holden Caulfield or Sergeant X. This is the first time, however, that Salinger has created a female for tracing out the pattern. Perhaps it was inevitable that first readers of "Franny" would assume that she was pregnant, thus neatly explaining for themselves her nausea and fainting. It is, however, quite clear that her sickness is of the spirit. But, one might well ask, if Franny has had the kind of religious and spiritual education which Salinger depicts as inevitable for one growing up in the Glass household, why should she encounter a spiritual crisis with which she cannot cope at this time in her life? The answer seems to be, as suggested by Zooey, that it is precisely this early religious initiation that has somehow brought on the crisis. Franny is suffering from an excess of piety — an excess which is dehumanizing her and cutting her off from (in Hawthorne's words again) the "magnetic chain of humanity." When speaking of the phony poets at her school, whose poems are just some kind of "terribly fascinating, syntaxy *droppings,*" she exclaims: "I'm sick of just liking people." And she later cries out, "I'm just sick of ego, ego, ego. My own and everybody else's." Through Zooey, she learns that her use of the Jesus prayer has handicapped rather than helped her spiritually, because of her distorted notions of Jesus. In saying the Jesus prayer, she has been trying to lay up spiritual treasures for herself much like the people she criticizes are trying, in one way or another, to lay up material or intellectual treasures for themselves. "This is God's universe," Zooey tells Franny, "not yours." And he asks: ". . . who in the Bible besides Jesus knew — *knew* — that we're carrying the Kingdom of Heaven around with us, *inside,* where we're all too goddam stupid and sentimental and unimaginative to look?" The only reason to say the Jesus prayer is to develop "Christ-Consciousness" — "*Not* to set up some little cozy, holier-than-thou trysting place with some sticky, adorable divine *per*sonage."

Shocked — or blasted — out of her alienating, self-righteous piety, Franny is prepared for the final insight that Zooey has to give her, an insight that Seymour passed along to Zooey, in preparing for one of the radio shows (all the Glass children have appeared on a radio program entitled "It's a Wise Child"). Seymour told the reluctant Zooey that he should shine his shoes for "the Fat Lady." Over the years, the image of the Fat Lady – sitting on a porch, swatting flies, with a case of cancer, her radio going full blast – has grown in Zooey's mind into an image of suffering humanity, an embodiment, ultimately, of Christ. Zooey tells Franny: "There isn't anyone *any*where that isn't Seymour's Fat Lady. Don't you know that? . . . And don't you know – *listen* to me, now – *don't you know who that Fat Lady really is?* . . . Ah, buddy, Ah, buddy. It's Christ Himself. Christ Himself, buddy." This is the intuitive knowledge that at last replaces Franny's revulsion with joy, and brings a smile to her lips – the smile of return.

Though "Zooey" is the story of Franny's road back, it is also in some sense the story of Zooey's supreme effort. For in truth, Zooey understands Franny so well because he has "been there" himself; indeed, he makes the journey frequently, but is always able to return – on his own power. Both he and Franny have, he says, been made into freaks by their older brothers, Seymour and Buddy. The moment that Zooey gets into a room with somebody, he tells Franny, "I either turn into a goddam *seer* or a human hatpin. The Prince of Bores." He sees the phoniness of his television associates – but he has learned to like them, and even the things about them that at first repel. But he exclaims to Franny, "I'm sick to death of being the heavy in everybody's life." The act of spiritual resurrection that he performs for Franny is frighteningly exhausting – his fresh shirt is drenched with sweat and he himself profoundly exhausted. The effort takes such toll because he is renewing himself at the same time he is saving Franny.

When Zooey is introduced, we are told (by Buddy, the self-suppressed narrator) that there is superimposed on his face an "undiminishable . . . joy." As Zooey sits in the bathtub in the opening scene, he is returning to the source of both his spiritual tension and his intuitive wisdom, Seymour and Buddy, via Buddy's four-year-old letter. In the letter Buddy describes a recent experience at the supermarket: when he asked a little girl the names of her two boyfriends, the little girl replied, "Bobby and Dorothy." The little girl, Buddy saw, instinctively realized what Seymour once told him, ". . . that all legitimate religious study *must* lead to unlearning the differences, the illusory differences, between boys and girls, animals and stones, day and night, heat and cold." Later, while talking in the living room with Franny, Zooey himself glances out the drapeless windows and sees a little drama in progress: a small girl in a red tam is hiding behind a tree from her dog wearing a green collar; the "anguish of separation" is followed by the "joy of reunion." From this little but intensely suggestive vignette Zooey draws the inspiration to force Franny to see the anguish of her own separation and the need for a reunion of joy. In the final scene of the story, when Zooey goes into Seymour's old room, he glances over the items tacked on an expanse of beaver-board – quotations culled from everywhere, from the *Bhagavad Gita* to Ring Lardner, from Epictetus and Marcus Aurelius to Kafka and Anna Karenina. From a brief communion with these and with Seymour's diary cards, Zooey gathers the strength to make the final and supreme effort to rescue Franny from her isolation.

The techniques introduced in *Franny and Zooey* are characteristic of Salinger's later work. The humor of *Catcher* has almost disappeared, and replacing the fast-moving and richly varied narrative sequence of the earlier novel is an almost static narrative pattern moving from one long conversation to another, interspersed with occasional monologues or individual readings of letters, diaries, or journals. This change no doubt accounts in part for the lack of popularity of these later works. But compensating somewhat for the loss of humor and variety are gains, perhaps, in particularity and profundity. The accretion of physical detail in these stories is sometimes astonishing – as, for example, when we are introduced to the contents of the Glass medicine cabinet. And the physical details are not excess baggage but functional, each object pulling its own weight. A major example is Zooey's cigar, which serves as material and substantial ballast both to his slight build and to his mystic tendencies of thought: his cigar keeps Zooey grounded. As for the profundity, these later stories explore not so much the phoniness of the world and the self (as *Catcher* did) but the other side of the coin, the sources of insight and stability that enable an individual to come to terms with himself and the world. Although whatever wisdom the books have must be, ultimately, attributed to Salinger, as he has dramatized it through the Glasses, there is great use made throughout of what might be called secondary sources; sometimes these books look like reading lists for courses in comparative religion, or indexes for religious encyclopedias. The narrator Buddy is a college teacher who lectures to the faculty once a week on Zen and Mahayana Buddhism. He and Seymour, Buddy's letter to Zooey reveals, wanted Franny and Zooey "to know who and what Jesus and Gautama and Lao-tse and Shankaracharya and Hui-neng and Sri Ramakrishna" were before finding out "too much" about Homer, Shakespeare, Blake, or Whitman. Of course this technique is not new to Salinger, but never before did it seem to threaten narrative or displace theme. Still, at his best Salinger renders this material functional, subordinate to the human drama he is portraying. Buddy says in his prologue to "Zooey": "I say that my current offering isn't a mystical story, or a religiously mystifying story, at all. *I* say it's a compound, or multiple, love story, pure and complicated." Salinger's later works must not be read as religious tracts, no matter how tempting the reading lists make such an interpretation. Zooey himself demonstrates the vast distance separating the cold printed words of the sages, however wise, and the warm human act of actual, breathing involvement with people when he turns from

Seymour's bulletin board of miscellaneous wisdom to tell Franny about the Fat Lady and the flies.

In the two stories of *Raise High the Roof Beam, Carpenters; and Seymour: An Introduction*, Buddy Glass remains the narrator throughout, and rather than suppressing himself, as in "Zooey," tends constantly to become his own main character. In "Raise High" Buddy is a soldier on leave to attend his brother's wedding in New York in 1942, but Seymour does not appear. The bride, Muriel, is left waiting at the church, to everybody's horror, but everything is made right when Seymour later elopes with her. The story itself is concerned, therefore, not so much with the wedding as with the reaction of a number of people, including Buddy, to Seymour's strange behavior. After a long wait at the church, and after the bride has left with her parents, Buddy gets caught in a taxicab with the bride's matron of honor and her lieutenant husband, with an aunt of the bride, and with a tiny deaf-mute who turns out to be the bride's father's uncle. The taxicab gets trapped by a parade and the conversation about Seymour lurches and languishes, taking on new life when the understandably upset matron of honor finds out that Buddy is a brother of the groom. The matron of honor divulges the information that she has previously garnered from the bride's mother (who has consulted her psychiatrist) that Seymour is schizoid and, probably, a latent homosexual. When he was a boy, the matron of honor relates with some relish, he struck one of the girls on the Glass children's radio program, "It's a Wise Child" – the blow necessitating nine stitches in the face of the girl, now a famous actress. When the occupants of the taxi finally get out to find a cold drink, the place they try is closed and Buddy brings them all up to his and Seymour's nearby apartment, where they marvel over the pictures of the Glass prodigies, drink some hastily concocted Tom Collinses, and prod Buddy with slightly hostile questions about his brother and himself. When they discover by phone that the elopement has set things right, the hostility somewhat abates and the unwanted guests depart.

"Raise High" is ingeniously constructed to focus on a series of superficially "normal" and negative attitudes toward Seymour by trapping them in a frame — the narrator's commentary — of sympathetic and understanding exploration of Seymour's real character. By this running contrast, the views tossed out by the matron of honor and assented to generally by her listeners are shown to be vacuous, inane, and almost brutally gross. Buddy prefaces his story with the Taoist tale of the horse judge who picked a superlative horse but did not know its color or sex, illustrating the difference in perceiving essentials and externals. Buddy's story of the wedding is, in a sense, an elaboration of this tale — the wedding guests never arrive beyond the externals in judging Seymour; Buddy sees into the essentials — the "spiritual mechanism" itself. He has, of course, certain advantages. He has known Seymour a long time; he has at hand Seymour's diary that can bring him up to date on Seymour's feelings about Muriel; and he has an unexpected ally — the tiny deaf-mute, who seems in some mysterious, mystic way to be a judge of superlative horses himself. This little man functions as some kind of saint or guru who remains throughout sublimely, blissfully disengaged. The one verbal response he makes (in writing) in reply to the invitation to get out of the taxi with the others for a drink, is — characteristically — "Delighted." He is life's delighted man, bestowing his blessing with his smile and his cigar on all the anguished people around him. He is the one guest that remains as the others leave, to lend his understanding but unhearing ear to Buddy's explanation of Seymour's behavior. The boy Seymour struck Charlotte Mayhew with a rock, Buddy tells the tiny man, "because she looked so beautiful sitting there in the middle of the driveway with Boo Boo's cat." The deaf-mute grins and agrees. He is the one guest who can grasp this paradox of the "spiritual mechanism."

Seymour's diary, which Buddy reads in the bathroom, reveals with some fullness the relationship between Seymour and Muriel. It is clear that he sees her as a steadying force in his own highly strung, keyed-up existence. He loves her, therefore, for those qualities he himself does not possess – her somewhat simple tastes and broad, low-keyed emotional responses. "How I love and need her undiscriminating heart," he writes; and "How I worship her simplicity, her terrible honesty. How I rely on it." In short, Seymour sees beyond the vulgar externals of Muriel to her potential "spiritual mechanism." Although he senses that he does not make her "really happy," his consolation is that she has a "basically undeviating love for the institution of marriage itself." Muriel's mother, however, is a different matter. Muriel has told her how Seymour got the scars on his wrist (this is the only reference to a previous attempt at suicide in the Glass stories), and Mrs. Fedder is disturbed because Seymour has said once at dinner that he would like to be a dead cat (he explains later to Muriel that "in Zen Buddhism a master was once asked what was the most valuable thing in the world, and the master answered that a dead cat was, because no one could put a price on it"). Although Mrs. Fedder possesses no "understanding or taste for the main current of poetry that flows through things, all things," Seymour still asserts "I love her. I find her unimaginably brave."

At one of the Fedder dinner parties, Seymour repeats a remark he'd made as a youngster on the radio, that Lincoln at Gettysburg should have remained silent and shaken his fist at the audience. Mrs. Fedder's psychiatrist tells Seymour he is a perfectionist and explains to him the "virtues of living the imperfect life, of accepting one's own and others' weaknesses." Seymour writes in his diary: "I agree with him, but only in theory. I'll champion indiscrimination till doomsday, on the ground that it leads to health and a kind of very real, enviable happiness. *Followed purely,* it's the way of the Tao, and undoubtedly the highest way. But for a discriminating man to achieve this, it would mean that he would have to dispossess himself of poetry, go *beyond* poetry." *Followed purely* — there is the rub, and the irony. Seymour is the purest of its actual followers in the story (compare, for example, the matron of honor and other wedding guests), and yet he recognizes himself that he falls short. Seymour's "fault" is his keen attunement to the "current of poetry that flows through things." "I have scars on my hands from touching certain people," he writes, in a bizarre confession of intimate sensitivity. "I'm a kind of paranoic in reverse. I suspect people of plotting to make me happy." They are plotting, of course, with their psychiatrists, to adjust Seymour to *their* imperfections, their hypocrisies and phoniness, as they cannot adjust to his shortcomings, his revulsions and ecstasies. The result, ultimately, will be his suicide — not a gesture of defiance and contempt, but a gesture of sad capitulation.

"Seymour: An Introduction" continues the exploration of the saint of the Glass family, but for the first time Salinger frees himself from the restrictive demands of dramatizing in detail a small segment in time (the day of the wedding, or the day of the suicide) and ranges freely over the whole of Seymour's biography. Or rather, Buddy Glass, novelist and teacher, so ranges, as he is the narrator. When Buddy surfaces briefly in that prologue to "Zooey," he says that what he is about to relate is less like a short story than a "prose home movie." This metaphor seems apt for "Seymour: An Introduction." Buddy presents a series of miscellaneous portraits of Seymour without bothering to provide a narrative thread on which to hang them. The structure that he does provide has more to do with Buddy than with Seymour. In the opening pages of the story, Buddy presents to the reader an "unpretentious bouquet of very early-blooming parentheses: ((((())))).” The story that follows is full of parenthetical comments, in the form of intimate asides to the reader, about Buddy himself and about the agony of composition. Indeed, Buddy seems to be writing the story while he is in process of having some kind of nervous or spiritual breakdown (at one point he specifies acute hepatitis), and as his collapse becomes more evident, the story of Seymour becomes less coherent and at times fades to the background. But nevertheless, reconstruction of Seymour's story is excellent therapy, self-administered, for Buddy's ailing spirit; and he comes through, if not healed, at least reconciled to – even happy in – his fate. Buddy thus joins the gallery of Salinger characters – Holden, Sergeant X, Franny, and even Zooey – who suffer a sickness of the soul, but, through some marvelous renewal, survive. They all withdraw, but they also all return.

Seymour alone, among Salinger's suffering heroes, makes the ultimate withdrawal, and Buddy seems driven to explain why. After a long, rambling prologue, a kind of "thesaurus of undetached prefatory remarks" about himself, his reader, and his brother Seymour, Buddy begins a semi-systematic treatment of his subject. He presents Seymour the poet, Seymour the critic, and, finally, Seymour as a physical entity. Serving somewhat in the capacity of his brother's literary executor, Buddy has in his possession 184 of Seymour's short poems: they look "substantially like an English translation of a sort of double haiku." Seymour, Buddy assures us, will eventually stand with the three or four "*very* nearly nonexpendable" American poets. But since he is forbidden to present here the poems directly (by Seymour's wife, we are told in a footnote), Buddy paraphrases the two he considers best. A young married woman and mother who is having an affair returns home one night from a "tryst" and finds an inflated balloon on her bed. A young suburban widower sits on his lawn at night looking at the moon while a "bored white cat" comes up, rolls over, and bites his left hand. Buddy would be the first to admit that the poems lose something—a great deal—in "translation by paraphrase." But the pattern is clear: unsentimentalized minor moments of major illumination or epiphany; finely etched vignettes which reveal the "spiritual mechanism" beneath the externals.

As a critic, Seymour is represented through his commentary on a number of Buddy's stories, and the essence of his advice is summed up in two questions he tells Buddy he will be asked as a writer when he dies: "*Were most of your stars out? Were you busy writing your heart out?*" Although Seymour's questions, like his poems, cannot really be paraphrased, he seems to suggest that *insight* and *feeling*—in their deepest senses—must be involved in great writing; and for the reader they become those elusive, indefinable qualities that are profoundly moving and illuminating. A description of Seymour as a physical entity almost proves Buddy's undoing. As he moves through a catalogue of Seymour's physical characteristics—hair, ears, eyes, nose, voice, skin, clothes—he becomes progressively more intrusive and less coherent, at times, apparently, painfully near disintegration (for example, he announces after a brief passage on Seymour's ears, "I'm going to bed. . . . The hands are sweating, the bowels churning. The Integrated Man is simply not at home").

"Seymour: An Introduction" seems not so much a story as an assemblage of notes, observations, anecdotes, and irrelevancies ("blooming parentheses"), much like Buddy's (or Salinger's) journal, from which a story might one day be made. The Seymour that emerges is generally consistent with the Seymour we have come to know already; new material is presented, new complexities revealed, but no genuinely new dimensions are added to his portrait. In a way, then, the story is Buddy's, as we see him for the first time in all his agony of spirit attempting to retain and strengthen his grasp on the elusive truths lurking in Seymour's life. He seems in desperate need of them. He introduces himself at the beginning, with some irony, as an "ecstatically happy man"; and at the end, as he prepares to go to class, he realizes that "no single thing" he does is "more important than going into that awful Room 307." As Seymour once said, "all we do our whole lives is go from one little piece of Holy Ground to the next."

"Seymour: An Introduction" may be said to have the form that conceals form, with all the seeming irrelevancies deliberately designed to create an even greater than usual illusion of reality—the real reality (a technique, incidentally, not uncommon, as witness Dostoevski's "Notes from Underground" or Rilke's *The Notebook of Malte Laurids Brigge*). But, still, there is a lingering doubt about the author's control, a doubt that is somewhat reinforced by Buddy's recurrent resemblance to Salinger. Throughout the story, references are made, particularly to the works that Buddy has written, that force this identification. One of Buddy's works is clearly *The Catcher in the Rye,* two others are "Raise High the Roof Beam, Carpenters" (in which Buddy was narrator) and "A Perfect Day for Bananafish" (in which he was not), and still another is "Teddy" (Buddy even quotes from it). Such details as these and others do not, of course, prove anything, but they do suggest—and *just* suggest—that Salinger is revealing, however obliquely, his own loss of control and diffusion of talent.

Salinger's long silence after the appearance of "Seymour: An Introduction" in 1959 was ended in 1965 with the publication of another chapter in the Glass saga, "Hapworth 16, 1924." This story did nothing to reassure those who hoped for a return to the earlier brilliance of *Catcher in the Rye.* Indeed, it tended to accentuate those characteristics of the later work which most readers found disturbing—a tedious length, a humor often self-consciously cute, a muting of narrative in favor of philosophical asides. But in spite of its apparent defects, the story was an important addition to the life of the Glasses, particularly as it shed new light on the remarkable character of Seymour.

"Hapworth 16, 1924" opens with a brief note by Buddy Glass introducing a long, long letter—the entire body of the story—from seven-year-old Seymour at summer camp to his vaudeville-touring family. The letter is startling not only for its length (around 30,000 words) but also for its casually revealed assumptions. Seymour (as well as his five-year-old brother Buddy, with him at camp) is now in one of a sequence of appearances or incarnations about which he seems to have transcendent or superhuman knowledge. He confesses that a "vein of instability" runs through him "like some turbulent river"—a "troublesome instability" that remained uncorrected in his "previous two appearances." This revelation, together with his foreknowledge of his death at around thirty, is surely meant to shed light on his suicide in 1948, some twenty-four years after this letter was written. He says at one point: "I for one do not look forward to being distracted by charming lusts of thc body, quite day in and day out, for the few, blissful, remaining years allotted to me in this appearance."

Seymour's unusual knowledge of the past and insight into the future derive from "two, tantalizing, tiny portals" in his mind which have opened involuntarily and which give him foresight not only of his own life but also of the lives of others. At one point he has a "stunning glimpse" of Buddy, "quite bereft" of Seymour's "dubious, loving company," busily at work writing stories on his "very large, jet-black, very moving, gorgeous typewriter." The effect of such passages is difficult to describe or assess. They seem both preposterous and ironic.

Is Salinger pulling our leg? Or is he drawing a portrait of the seer and saint as a young man? Or is he seriously presenting his genuine belief alongside Seymour's? "Hapworth 16, 1924" ends with a long list of books that Seymour requests be sent to him at summer camp. The list ranges from the complete works of Dickens and Tolstoi to *The Gayatri Prayer* and Porter Smith's *Chinese Materia Medica*. Few men could get through this interminable reading list in a lifetime, let alone in a summer. And most readers are likely to be disturbed by the diffuseness and miscellaneousness of all the materials in this story, elements which seem to confirm the deterioration of talent detected in "Seymour: An Introduction."

Like Eliot or Melville, Salinger is full enough of quotations from literature and references to writers to suggest his own literary context and tradition. References range astonishingly through the poetry and religious literature of India, China, Japan, and throughout Western literature from Blake, Dostoevski, and Rilke to Kierkegaard and Kafka. But in spite of this wide scattering of interests and attractions, Salinger is not a Zen Buddhist or a philosopher or a poet. He is an American novelist writing in the American tradition. At one point in "Zooey," Buddy Glass says, significantly, that *The Great Gatsby* was his *Tom Sawyer* when he was twelve. The confession reveals a fundamental affinity for the native tradition.

Salinger is allied, in a basic way, to the joyful mysticism of Whitman, but he responds, too, to the mystical anguish of Emily Dickinson as well as to the macabre humor of Mark Twain. He no doubt finds much for himself in the idiom and prose rhythms of Ring Lardner, and he is attracted by F. Scott Fitzgerald's poetic style as well as his explorations of idealism and reality. From his own era, we might guess that his sympathies would be attracted to Wright Morris' probing of time, and John Updike's examination of the relation of spirit and matter. But the basic patterns of his novels, the patterns of withdrawal and return, of the search for the ideal and the discovery of self, of the fall from innocence and the acknowledgment of complicity, are also the basic patterns of Hawthorne and Melville, though these are two writers that he does not mention. He does refer to Eliot, but never with enthusiasm; and though he did not entirely escape the wasteland vision, it is clear that his tastes (and his themes) are more closely akin to affirmative poetry of the mystical tradition.

Something of a paradox emerges from this alignment of American writers with Salinger—and this paradox brings us close to the heart of Salinger's achievement. Salinger's work may be described, metaphorically, as a cry of mystical joy transcendent over the modern wasteland and its agony. Two lines from Whitman's "Song of Myself" may suggest the thematic center of Salinger's work. The first (which he quotes in "The Inverted Forest"): "I am the man, I suffer'd, I was there." The second: "It is not chaos or death—it is form, union, plan—it is eternal life—it is Happiness." Translated into the modern idiom of Salinger, these basic feelings might be reconstructed: although modern man feels "his mind dislodge itself and teeter, like insecure luggage on an overhead rack," he must, to maintain his sanity, develop his understanding "for the main current of poetry that flows through things, all things." Like Seymour, he must go his appointed rounds, realizing that "all we do our whole lives is go from one little piece of Holy Ground to the next."

Although Salinger's total creative production, to date, has been relatively small, his impact and influence—and his artistic achievement—have been enormous. No serious history of post-World War II American fiction can be written without awarding him a place in the first rank, and even, perhaps, the pre-eminent position.

Selected Bibliography

Works of J. D. Salinger

UNCOLLECTED SHORT STORIES

"The Young Folks," *Story*, 16:26–30 (March–April 1940).

"Go See Eddie," *University of Kansas City Review*, 7:121–24 (December 1940).

"The Hang of It," *Collier's*, 108:22 (July 12, 1941).

"The Heart of a Broken Story," *Esquire*, 16:32, 131–33 (September 1941).

"The Long Debut of Lois Taggett," *Story*, 21:28–34 (September–October 1942). Reprinted in *Story: The Fiction of the Forties*, edited by Whit and Hallie S. Burnett. New York: Dutton, 1949. Pp. 153–62.

"Personal Notes on an Infantryman," *Collier's*, 110:96 (December 12, 1942).

"The Varioni Brothers," *Saturday Evening Post*, 216:12–13, 76–77 (July 17, 1943).

"Both Parties Concerned," *Saturday Evening Post*, 216:14, 47–48 (February 26, 1944).

"Soft-Boiled Sergeant," *Saturday Evening Post*, 216:18, 82, 84–85 (April 15, 1944).

"Last Day of the Last Furlough," *Saturday Evening Post*, 217:26–27, 61–62, 64 (July 15, 1944).

"Once a Week Won't Kill You," *Story*, 25:23–27 (November–December 1944).

"Elaine," *Story*, 26:38–47 (March–April 1945).

"A Boy in France," *Saturday Evening Post*, 217:21, 92 (March 31, 1945).

"This Sandwich Has No Mayonnaise," *Esquire*, 25:54–56, 147–49 (October 1945). Reprinted in *The Armchair Esquire*, edited by Arnold Gingrich and L. Rush Hills. New York: Putnam, 1958. Pp. 187–97.

"The Stranger," *Collier's*, 116:18, 77 (December 1, 1945).

"I'm Crazy," *Collier's*, 116:36, 48, 51 (December 22, 1945).

"Slight Rebellion off Madison," *New Yorker*, 22:76–79 (December 21, 1946).

"A Young Girl in 1941 with No Waist at All," *Mademoiselle*, 25:222–23, 292–302 (May 1947).

"The Inverted Forest," *Cosmopolitan*, 123:73–80, 85–86, 88, 90, 92, 95–96, 98, 100, 102, 107, 109 (December 1947). Reprinted in *Cosmopolitan*, 150:111–32 (March 1961).

"A Girl I Knew," *Good Housekeeping*, 126:37, 186, 188, 191–96 (February 1948). Reprinted in *Best American Short Stories of 1949; and the Yearbook of the American Short Story*, edited by Martha J. Foley. Boston: Houghton Mifflin, 1949. Pp. 248–60.
"Blue Melody," *Cosmopolitan*, 125:51, 112–19 (September 1948).
"Hapworth 16, 1924," *New Yorker*, 41:32–113 (June 19, 1965).

NOVELS AND COLLECTIONS OF SHORT STORIES

The Catcher in the Rye. Boston: Little, Brown, 1951.
Nine Stories. Boston: Little, Brown, 1953. (Contains the following stories which first appeared as indicated: "A Perfect Day for Bananafish," *New Yorker*, 23:21–25 (January 31, 1948); "Uncle Wiggily in Connecticut," *New Yorker*, 24:30–36 (March 20, 1948); "Just before the War with the Eskimos," *New Yorker*, 24:37–40, 42, 44, 46 (June 5, 1948); "The Laughing Man," *New Yorker*, 25:27–32 (March 19, 1949); "Down at the Dinghy," *Harper's*, 198:87–91 (April 1949); "For Esmé — with Love and Squalor," *New Yorker*, 26:28–36 (April 8, 1950); "Pretty Mouth and Green My Eyes," *New Yorker*, 27:20–24 (July 14, 1951); "De Daumier-Smith's Blue Period," *World Review* (London), May 1952, pp. 33–48; "Teddy," *New Yorker*, 28:26–36, 38 (January 31, 1953).)
Franny and Zooey. Boston: Little, Brown, 1961. (Contains the following stories which first appeared as indicated: "Franny," *New Yorker*, 30:24–32, 35–43 (January 29, 1955); "Zooey," *New Yorker*, 33:32–42, 44–139 (May 4, 1957).)
Raise High the Roof Beam, Carpenters; and Seymour: An Introduction. Boston: Little, Brown, 1963. (Contains the following stories which first appeared as indicated: "Raise High the Roof Beam, Carpenters," *New Yorker*, 31:51–58, 60–116 (November 19, 1955); "Seymour: An Introduction," *New Yorker*, 35:42–52, 54–111 (June 6, 1959).)

CURRENT AMERICAN REPRINTS

The Catcher in the Rye. New York: Bantam Books. $.75.
Nine Stories. New York: Bantam Books. $.75.
Franny and Zooey. New York: Bantam Books. $.75.
Raise High the Roof Beam, Carpenters; and Seymour: An Introduction. New York: Bantam Books. $.75.

Bibliography

Fiene, Donald F. "J. D. Salinger: A Bibliography," *Wisconsin Studies in Contemporary Literature*, 4:109–49 (Winter 1963).

Critical and Biographical Studies

Belcher, William F., and James W. Lee, eds. *J. D. Salinger and the Critics.* Belmont, Calif.: Wadsworth Publishing Company, 1962. (Contains 24 essays by a variety of critics.)

French, Warren. *J. D. Salinger.* New York: Twayne, 1963.

Grunwald, Henry Anatole, ed. *Salinger: A Critical and Personal Portrait.* New York: Harper, 1962. (A large selection of articles by various critics.)

Gwynne, Frederick L., and Joseph L. Blotner. *The Fiction of J. D. Salinger.* Pittsburgh: University of Pittsburgh Press, 1958.

Laser, Marvin, and Norman Fruman, eds. *Studies in J. D. Salinger: Reviews, Essays, and Critiques of The Catcher in the Rye and Other Fiction.* New York: Odyssey Press, 1963.

Marsden, Malcolm M., ed. *If You Really Want to Know: A Catcher Casebook.* Chicago: Scott, Foresman, 1963.

Simonson, Harold P., and Philip E. Hager, eds. *Salinger's "Catcher in the Rye": Clamor vs. Criticism.* Boston: D. C. Heath and Company, 1963.

Wisconsin Studies in Contemporary Literature. Special Number: Salinger. 4:1–160 (Winter 1963).

Miller

literature

UNIVERSITY OF MINNESOTA PAMPHLETS ON AMERICAN WRITERS

William Van O'Connor, Allen Tate, Leonard Unger, and Robert Penn Warren, editors. Willard Thorp, Karl Shapiro, and Philip Rahv, advisers

1.	ERNEST HEMINGWAY	by Philip Young
2.	ROBERT FROST	by Lawrance Thompson
3.	WILLIAM FAULKNER	by William Van O'Connor
4.	HENRY JAMES	by Leon Edel
5.	MARK TWAIN	by Lewis Leary
6.	THOMAS WOLFE	by C. Hugh Holman
7.	RECENT AMERICAN DRAMA	by Alan S. Downer
8.	T. S. ELIOT	by Leonard Unger
9.	WALT WHITMAN	by Richard Chase
10.	GERTRUDE STEIN	by Frederick J. Hoffman
11.	WALLACE STEVENS	by William Y. Tindall
12.	EDITH WHARTON	by Louis Auchincloss
13.	HERMAN MELVILLE	by Leon Howard
14.	THE AMERICAN SHORT STORY	by Danforth Ross
15.	F. SCOTT FITZGERALD	by Charles E. Shain
16.	RECENT AMERICAN POETRY	by Glauco Cambon
17.	EDWIN ARLINGTON ROBINSON	by Louis Coxe
18.	JOHN CROWE RANSOM	by John L. Stewart
19.	BENJAMIN FRANKLIN	by Theodore Hornberger
20.	JOHN DOS PASSOS	by Robert Gorham Davis
21.	NATHANAEL WEST	by Stanley Edgar Hyman
22.	RECENT AMERICAN NOVELISTS	by Jack Ludwig
23.	NATHANIEL HAWTHORNE	by Hyatt H. Waggoner
24.	WILLIAM CARLOS WILLIAMS	by John Malcolm Brinnin
25.	WASHINGTON IRVING	by Lewis Leary
26.	EZRA POUND	by William Van O'Connor
27.	SINCLAIR LEWIS	by Mark Schorer
28.	KATHERINE ANNE PORTER	by Ray B. West, Jr.
29.	JAMES T. FARRELL	by Edgar M. Branch
30.	THEODORE ROETHKE	by Ralph J. Mills, Jr.
31.	REINHOLD NIEBUHR	by Nathan A. Scott, Jr.
32.	LITTLE MAGAZINES	by Reed Whittemore
33.	ELLEN GLASGOW	by Louis Auchincloss
34.	THORNTON WILDER	by Bernard Grebanier
35.	HENRY WADSWORTH LONGFELLOW	by Edward Hirsh
36.	WILLA CATHER	by Dorothy Van Ghent
37.	AMBROSE BIERCE	by Robert A. Wiggins
38.	CONRAD AIKEN	by Reuel Denney
39.	ALLEN TATE	by George Hemphill
40.	ARTHUR MILLER	by Robert Hogan
41.	RALPH WALDO EMERSON	by Josephine Miles
42.	AMERICAN HUMORISTS	by Willard Thorp
43.	SHERWOOD ANDERSON	by Brom Weber
44.	ROBERT PENN WARREN	by Paul West
45.	EUGENE O'NEILL	by John Gassner
46.	JOHN P. MARQUAND	by C. Hugh Holman
47.	HART CRANE	by Monroe K. Spears
48.	JAMES FENIMORE COOPER	by Robert E. Spiller
49.	RING LARDNER	by Otto Friedrich
50.	MARIANNE MOORE	by Jean Garrigue
51.	J. D. SALINGER	by James E. Miller, Jr.
52.	EDWARD TAYLOR	by Donald E. Stanford
53.	TENNESSEE WILLIAMS	by Gerald Weales

EACH PAMPHLET, 65 CENTS

UNIVERSITY OF MINNESOTA PRESS, Minneapolis, Minnesota 55455, U.S.A.
Distributed to high schools in the United States by Webster Division
McGRAW-HILL BOOK COMPANY
St. Louis New York San Francisco Dallas